The UNITED STATES PRESIDENTS

Benjamin HARRISON

Megan M. Gunderson

Big Buddy Books
An Imprint of Abdo Publishing
abdopublishing.com

abdopublishing.com

Published by Abdo Publishing, a division of ABDO, PO Box 398166, Minneapolis, Minnesota 55439. Copyright © 2017 by Abdo Consulting Group, Inc. International copyrights reserved in all countries. No part of this book may be reproduced in any form without written permission from the publisher. Big Buddy Books™ is a trademark and logo of Abdo Publishing.

Printed in the United States of America, North Mankato, Minnesota
062016
092016

 THIS BOOK CONTAINS
RECYCLED MATERIALS

Design: Sarah DeYoung, Mighty Media, Inc.
Production: Mighty Media, Inc.
Editor: Lauren Kukla
Cover Photograph: Getty Images
Interior Photographs: Alamy (pp. 7, 15, 21, 29); Library of Congress (pp. 5, 6, 7, 9, 11, 17, 25, 27); National Archives (p. 25); Picture History (pp. 13, 19, 23)

Cataloging-in-Publication Data

Names: Gunderson, Megan M., author.
Title: Benjamin Harrison / by Megan M. Gunderson.
Description: Minneapolis, MN : Abdo Publishing, [2017] | Series: United States presidents | Includes bibliographical references and index.
Identifiers: LCCN 2015044094 | ISBN 9781680780970 (lib. bdg.) | ISBN 9781680775174 (ebook)
Subjects: LCSH: Harrison, Benjamin, 1833-1901--Juvenile literature. 2. Presidents--United States--Biography--Juvenile literature. | United States--Politics and Government--1889-1893--Juvenile literature.
Classification: DDC 973.8/6092092 [B]--dc23
LC record available at http://lccn.loc.gov/2015044094

Contents

Benjamin Harrison

Benjamin Harrison was the twenty-third president of the United States. He came from a long line of American leaders. Harrison's grandfather was William H. Harrison. He was the ninth US president. Harrison's father served as a congressman.

In 1889, Harrison became president. He served a single term. During Harrison's presidency, six new states joined the United States. After his term, Harrison became a popular public speaker.

Timeline

1833

On August 20, Benjamin Harrison was born in North Bend, Ohio.

1857

Harrison was elected city **attorney** of Indianapolis, Indiana.

1880

Harrison won election to the US Senate.

1888

Harrison beat President Grover Cleveland in the presidential election.

1892

In November, Harrison lost reelection to Cleveland.

1889

On March 4, Harrison became the twenty-third US president.

1901

On March 13, Benjamin Harrison died.

Ohio Childhood

Benjamin Harrison was born in North Bend, Ohio, on August 20, 1833. Ben's parents were John Scott and Elizabeth Irwin Harrison.

At 14, Ben went to school in Cincinnati, Ohio. Then, in 1850, he went to college in Oxford, Ohio.

★ **FAST FACTS** ★

Born: August 20, 1833

Wives: Caroline Lavinia "Carrie" Scott (1832–1892), Mary Scott Lord Dimmick (1858–1948)

Children: four

Political Party: Republican

Age of Inauguration: 55

Years Served: 1889–1893

Vice President: Levi P. Morton

Died: March 13, 1901, age 67

Ben grew up on a farm called The Point. It sat on a point of land where the Ohio and Miami Rivers meet.

Life as a Lawyer

Harrison **graduated** from college in 1852. He then moved to Cincinnati to study law. In 1853, he married Caroline Lavinia "Carrie" Scott. The couple moved to Indianapolis, Indiana, in 1854. That same year, Harrison became a **lawyer**.

In 1855, William Wallace invited Harrison to become his law **partner**. Meanwhile, the Harrisons had three children. Sadly, the youngest died at birth.

While Harrison worked hard to provide for his family, Mrs. Harrison cared for the children. She also volunteered in the community and at church.

The Civil War

During this time, slavery split the nation. Most people in the North were against slavery. Many Southerners were in favor of it.

Harrison was against slavery. **Republicans** also opposed slavery. So, Harrison joined the Republican Party. He was elected city **attorney** of Indianapolis in 1857.

In 1861, Southern states began leaving the **Union**. They formed the **Confederate States of America**. The **American Civil War** began on April 12, 1861. Harrison joined the Union army.

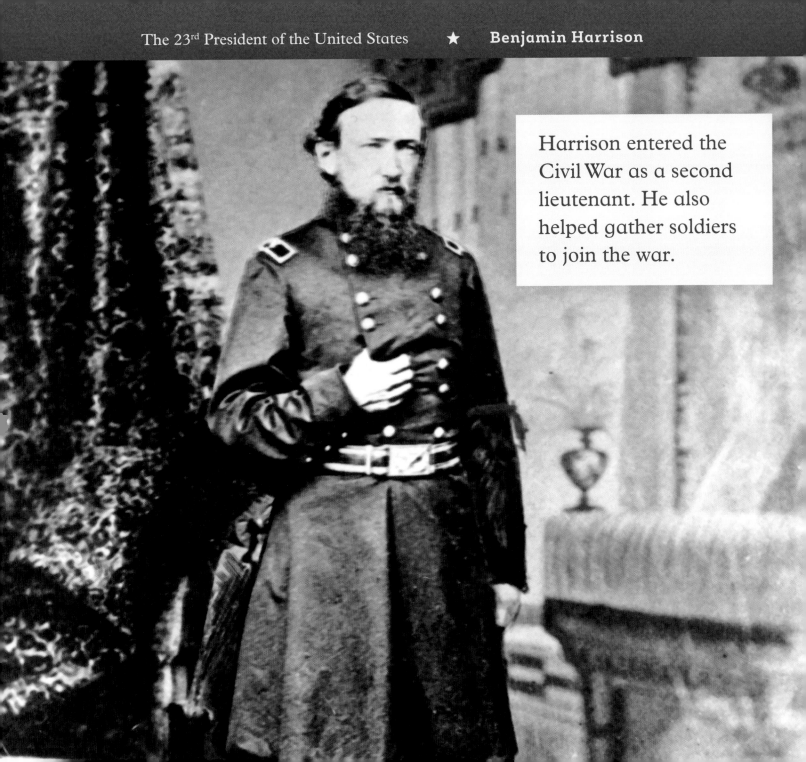

Harrison entered the Civil War as a second lieutenant. He also helped gather soldiers to join the war.

Harrison quickly **impressed** the **Union** army's leaders. Indiana Governor Oliver P. Morton made Harrison a colonel. During the day, Colonel Harrison trained his men. At night, he studied battle plans.

In the military, Harrison learned to be a leader. He led his soldiers in many successful battles in Georgia. So, President Abraham Lincoln promoted Harrison to **brevet** brigadier general. Then in 1865, the **American Civil War** ended.

★ DID YOU KNOW? ★

Benjamin and William H. Harrison are the only grandfather and grandson in US history to become president.

Indianapolis newspapers praised Harrison's success at the Battle of Resaca in Georgia in May 1854.

Supporting Hayes

Following the war, Harrison returned to his law practice. Then, in 1876, the **Republicans** chose Harrison to run for governor of Indiana. However, he lost the election.

After losing, Harrison went on a speaking tour. He campaigned for Republican presidential **candidate** Rutherford B. Hayes. Harrison earned national attention for his energetic speaking.

Hayes won the election. Then, in 1879, President Hayes **appointed** Harrison to the Mississippi River Commission.

Rutherford B. Hayes established the Mississippi River Commission in 1879. The group studied navigation and flooding on the river.

Senator Harrison

In 1880, Harrison won election to the US Senate. So, he and his family moved to Washington, DC.

In the Senate, Harrison stood up for what he believed in. He worked for **civil service** improvements. And, he fought for rights for African Americans.

Harrison also spoke out against the Chinese Exclusion Act of 1882. However, this law to limit Chinese **immigration** still passed. Harrison did not win reelection in 1887.

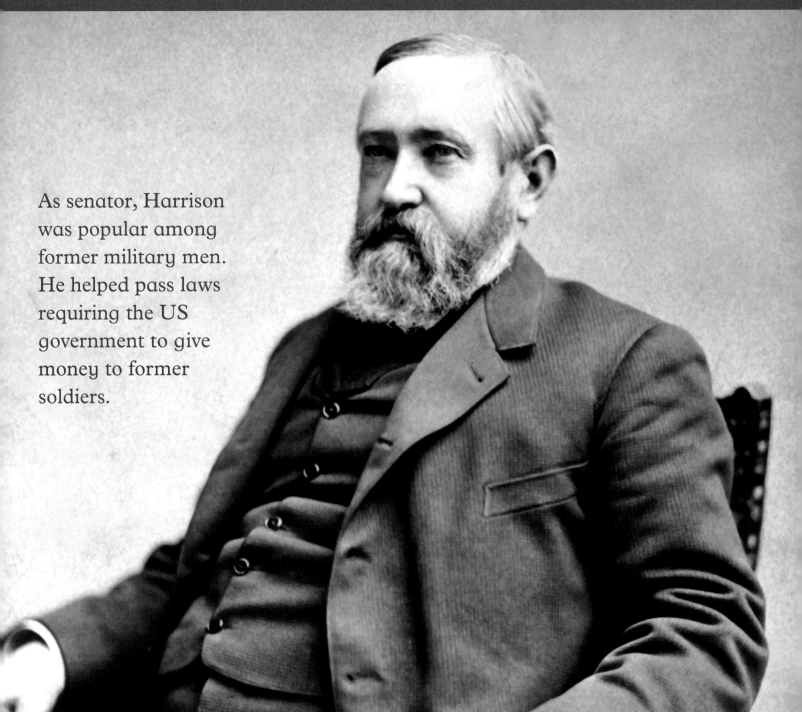

As senator, Harrison was popular among former military men. He helped pass laws requiring the US government to give money to former soldiers.

The Election of 1888

In 1888, the **Republicans** selected Harrison to run for president. His speaking skills and military service made him an excellent choice. **Democratic** president Grover Cleveland was running for reelection.

The election was very unusual. Cleveland earned more than 90,000 more **popular votes** than Harrison. However, Harrison won 233 **electoral votes**. Cleveland received only 168. Harrison won the election!

President Harrison became president on March 4, 1889.

President Harrison

As president, Harrison focused on helping US businesses. He built **relationships** with other countries. He also approved important bills.

One bill provided money to **veterans** of the **American Civil War** who could no longer work. Another bill required the government to coin more silver. This created more usable money.

Another important bill was the Sherman Antitrust Act. At the time, companies that sold the same product could join together. This meant there would be no competition between

PRESIDENT HARRISON'S CABINET

March 4, 1889–March 4, 1893

★ **STATE:** James G. Blaine, John W. Foster (from June 29, 1892)

★ **TREASURY:** William Windom, Charles Foster (from February 24, 1891)

★ **WAR:** Redfield Proctor, Stephen B. Elkins (from December 24, 1891)

★ **NAVY:** Benjamin F. Tracy

★ **ATTORNEY GENERAL:** William H.H. Miller

★ **INTERIOR:** John W. Noble

★ **AGRICULTURE:** Jeremiah M. Rusk

Harrison (*center*) with his cabinet

businesses. Then, they could charge higher prices for their products. The act banned these unions.

Other bills Harrison worked for did not pass. Two would have given more rights and protection to African Americans.

Meanwhile, six new states joined the United States during Harrison's presidency. The new states were North Dakota, South Dakota, Montana, Washington, Wyoming, and Idaho.

★ SUPREME COURT ★ APPOINTMENTS

David J. Brewer: 1890

Henry B. Brown: 1891

George Shiras Jr.: 1892

Howell E. Jackson: 1893

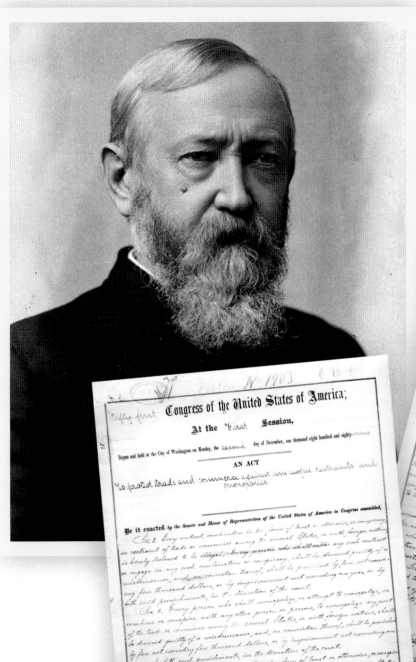

President Harrison
signed the Sherman
Antitrust Act into law
on July 2, 1890.

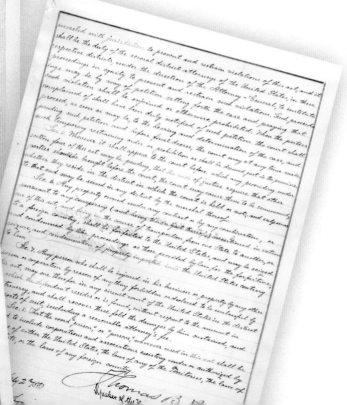

The Election of 1892

In 1892, President Harrison ran for reelection. The **Democratic** Party **nominated** former president Grover Cleveland. Mrs. Harrison was very ill during the campaign. So, President Harrison did not travel a lot to make speeches. Out of respect for Harrison, neither did Cleveland.

Then on October 25, Caroline Harrison died. Two weeks later, President Harrison lost the election. Cleveland won with 277 **electoral votes**. Harrison received 145 votes.

Grover
Cleveland
is the only
US president
to serve two
terms that
were not in
a row.

Back to Indiana

After the election, Harrison returned home to Indiana. Then on April 6, 1896, he married Mary Scott Lord Dimmick. The couple had one daughter. Meanwhile, Harrison practiced law and wrote. On March 13, 1901, Harrison died.

Benjamin Harrison was a great public speaker. He worked for African-American rights. Harrison is remembered as a leader who always stood up for his beliefs.

Harrison's Indianapolis home is still a national historic landmark.

Office of the President

Branches of Government

The US government has three branches. They are the executive, legislative, and judicial branches. Each branch has some power over the others. This is called a system of checks and balances.

★ **Executive Branch**

The executive branch enforces laws. It is made up of the president, the vice president, and the president's cabinet. The president represents the United States around the world. He or she also signs bills into law and leads the military.

★ **Legislative Branch**

The legislative branch makes laws, maintains the military, and regulates trade. It also has the power to declare war. This branch includes the Senate and the House of Representatives. Together, these two houses form Congress.

★ **Judicial Branch**

The judicial branch interprets laws. It is made up of district courts, courts of appeals, and the Supreme Court. District courts try cases. Sometimes people disagree with a trial's outcome. Then he or she may appeal. If a court of appeals supports the ruling, a person may appeal to the Supreme Court.

Qualifications for Office

To be president, a candidate must be at least 35 years old. The person must be a natural-born US citizen. He or she must also have lived in the United States for at least 14 years.

Electoral College

The US presidential election is an indirect election. Voters from each state choose electors. These electors represent their state in the Electoral College. Each elector has one electoral vote. Electors cast their vote for the candidate with the highest number of votes from people in their state. A candidate must receive the majority of Electoral College votes to win.

Term of Office

Each president may be elected to two four-year terms. The presidential election is held on the Tuesday after the first Monday in November. The president is sworn in on January 20 of the following year. At that time, he or she takes the oath of office.
It states:

I do solemnly swear (or affirm) that I will faithfully execute the office of President of the United States, and will to the best of my ability, preserve, protect and defend the Constitution of the United States.

31

Line of Succession

The Presidential Succession Act of 1947 states who becomes president if the president cannot serve. The vice president is first in the line. Next are the Speaker of the House and the President Pro Tempore of the Senate. It may happen that none of these individuals is able to serve. Then the office falls to the president's cabinet members. They would take office in the order in which each department was created:

Secretary of State

Secretary of the Treasury

Secretary of Defense

Attorney General

Secretary of the Interior

Secretary of Agriculture

Secretary of Commerce

Secretary of Labor

Secretary of Health and Human Services

Secretary of Housing and Urban Development

Secretary of Transportation

Secretary of Energy

Secretary of Education

Secretary of Veterans Affairs

Secretary of Homeland Security

Benefits

★ While in office, the president receives a salary. It is $400,000 per year. He or she lives in the White House. The president also has 24-hour Secret Service protection.

★ The president may travel on a Boeing 747 jet. This special jet is called Air Force One. It can hold 70 passengers. It has kitchens, a dining room, sleeping areas, and more. Air Force One can fly halfway around the world before needing to refuel. It can even refuel in flight!

★ When the president travels by car, he or she uses Cadillac One. It is a Cadillac Deville that has been modified. The car has heavy armor and communications systems. The president may even take Cadillac One along when visiting other countries.

★ The president also travels on a helicopter. It is called Marine One. It may also be taken along when the president visits other countries.

★ Sometimes the president needs to get away with family and friends. Camp David is the official presidential retreat. It is located in Maryland. The US Navy maintains the retreat. The US Marine Corps keeps it secure. The camp offers swimming, tennis, golf, and hiking.

★ When the president leaves office, he or she receives lifetime Secret Service protection. He or she also receives a yearly pension of $203,700. The former president also receives money for office space, supplies, and staff.

PRESIDENTS AND THEIR TERMS

PRESIDENT	PARTY	TOOK OFFICE	LEFT OFFICE	TERMS SERVED	VICE PRESIDENT
George Washington	None	April 30, 1789	March 4, 1797	Two	John Adams
John Adams	Federalist	March 4, 1797	March 4, 1801	One	Thomas Jefferson
Thomas Jefferson	Democratic-Republican	March 4, 1801	March 4, 1809	Two	Aaron Burr, George Clinton
James Madison	Democratic-Republican	March 4, 1809	March 4, 1817	Two	George Clinton, Elbridge Gerry
James Monroe	Democratic-Republican	March 4, 1817	March 4, 1825	Two	Daniel D. Tompkins
John Quincy Adams	Democratic-Republican	March 4, 1825	March 4, 1829	One	John C. Calhoun
Andrew Jackson	Democrat	March 4, 1829	March 4, 1837	Two	John C. Calhoun, Martin Van Buren
Martin Van Buren	Democrat	March 4, 1837	March 4, 1841	One	Richard M. Johnson
William H. Harrison	Whig	March 4, 1841	April 4, 1841	Died During First Term	John Tyler
John Tyler	Whig	April 6, 1841	March 4, 1845	Completed Harrison's Term	Office Vacant
James K. Polk	Democrat	March 4, 1845	March 4, 1849	One	George M. Dallas
Zachary Taylor	Whig	March 5, 1849	July 9, 1850	Died During First Term	Millard Fillmore

PRESIDENT	PARTY	TOOK OFFICE	LEFT OFFICE	TERMS SERVED	VICE PRESIDENT
Millard Fillmore	Whig	July 10, 1850	March 4, 1853	Completed Taylor's Term	Office Vacant
Franklin Pierce	Democrat	March 4, 1853	March 4, 1857	One	William R.D. King
James Buchanan	Democrat	March 4, 1857	March 4, 1861	One	John C. Breckinridge
Abraham Lincoln	Republican	March 4, 1861	April 15, 1865	Served One Term, Died During Second Term	Hannibal Hamlin, Andrew Johnson
Andrew Johnson	Democrat	April 15, 1865	March 4, 1869	Completed Lincoln's Second Term	Office Vacant
Ulysses S. Grant	Republican	March 4, 1869	March 4, 1877	Two	Schuyler Colfax, Henry Wilson
Rutherford B. Hayes	Republican	March 3, 1877	March 4, 1881	One	William A. Wheeler
James A. Garfield	Republican	March 4, 1881	September 19, 1881	Died During First Term	Chester Arthur
Chester Arthur	Republican	September 20, 1881	March 4, 1885	Completed Garfield's Term	Office Vacant
Grover Cleveland	Democrat	March 4, 1885	March 4, 1889	One	Thomas A. Hendricks
Benjamin Harrison	Republican	March 4, 1889	March 4, 1893	One	Levi P. Morton
Grover Cleveland	Democrat	March 4, 1893	March 4, 1897	One	Adlai E. Stevenson
William McKinley	Republican	March 4, 1897	September 14, 1901	Served One Term, Died During Second Term	Garret A. Hobart, Theodore Roosevelt

PRESIDENT	PARTY	TOOK OFFICE	LEFT OFFICE	TERMS SERVED	VICE PRESIDENT
Theodore Roosevelt	Republican	September 14, 1901	March 4, 1909	Completed McKinley's Second Term, Served One Term	Office Vacant, Charles Fairbanks
William Taft	Republican	March 4, 1909	March 4, 1913	One	James S. Sherman
Woodrow Wilson	Democrat	March 4, 1913	March 4, 1921	Two	Thomas R. Marshall
Warren G. Harding	Republican	March 4, 1921	August 2, 1923	Died During First Term	Calvin Coolidge
Calvin Coolidge	Republican	August 3, 1923	March 4, 1929	Completed Harding's Term, Served One Term	Office Vacant, Charles Dawes
Herbert Hoover	Republican	March 4, 1929	March 4, 1933	One	Charles Curtis
Franklin D. Roosevelt	Democrat	March 4, 1933	April 12, 1945	Served Three Terms, Died During Fourth Term	John Nance Garner, Henry A. Wallace, Harry S. Truman
Harry S. Truman	Democrat	April 12, 1945	January 20, 1953	Completed Roosevelt's Fourth Term, Served One Term	Office Vacant, Alben Barkley
Dwight D. Eisenhower	Republican	January 20, 1953	January 20, 1961	Two	Richard Nixon
John F. Kennedy	Democrat	January 20, 1961	November 22, 1963	Died During First Term	Lyndon B. Johnson
Lyndon B. Johnson	Democrat	November 22, 1963	January 20, 1969	Completed Kennedy's Term, Served One Term	Office Vacant, Hubert H. Humphrey
Richard Nixon	Republican	January 20, 1969	August 9, 1974	Completed First Term, Resigned During Second Term	Spiro T. Agnew, Gerald Ford

PRESIDENT	PARTY	TOOK OFFICE	LEFT OFFICE	TERMS SERVED	VICE PRESIDENT
Gerald Ford	Republican	August 9, 1974	January 20, 1977	Completed Nixon's Second Term	Nelson A. Rockefeller
Jimmy Carter	Democrat	January 20, 1977	January 20, 1981	One	Walter Mondale
Ronald Reagan	Republican	January 20, 1981	January 20, 1989	Two	George H.W. Bush
George H.W. Bush	Republican	January 20, 1989	January 20, 1993	One	Dan Quayle
Bill Clinton	Democrat	January 20, 1993	January 20, 2001	Two	Al Gore
George W. Bush	Republican	January 20, 2001	January 20, 2009	Two	Dick Cheney
Barack Obama	Democrat	January 20, 2009	January 20, 2017	Two	Joe Biden

"No other people have a government more worthy of their respect and love or a land so magnificent in extent." Benjamin Harrison

★ WRITE TO THE PRESIDENT ★

You may write to the president at:
The White House
1600 Pennsylvania Avenue NW
Washington, DC 20500

You may e-mail the president at:
comments@whitehouse.gov

37

Glossary

American Civil War—the war between the Northern and Southern states from 1861 to 1865.

appoint—to choose someone to do a job.

attorney—someone trained to give legal advice.

brevet—a military title given to an officer who has a higher rank than he or she is paid for.

candidate (KAN-duh-dayt)—a person who seeks a political office.

civil service—the part of the government that is responsible for matters not covered by the military, the courts, or the law.

Confederate States of America—the group of 11 Southern states that declared independence during the American Civil War.

Democrat—a member of the Democratic political party.

electoral vote—a vote cast by a member of the Electoral College for the candidate who received the most popular votes in his or her state.

graduate (GRA-juh-wayt)—to complete a level of schooling.

immigration—the act of leaving one's home and settling in a new country.

impress—to cause someone to feel admiration or respect.

lawyer (LAW-yuhr)—a person who gives people advice on laws or represents them in court.

nominate—to name as a possible winner.

partner—someone who is part of a group that jointly owns a business.

popular vote—the vote of the entire body of people with the right to vote.

relationship—the way people feel about or act toward one another.

Republican—a member of the Republican political party.

Union—the Northern states that remained part of the United States during the American Civil War.

veteran—a person who has served in the armed forces.

★ WEBSITES ★

To learn more about the US Presidents, visit **booklinks.abdopublishing.com**. These links are routinely monitored and updated to provide the most current information available.

Index